How I Lost the Love of My Life and Became Wealthy as a Result

How I Used The Law of Attraction to Unlock Health, Wealth, And Happiness

BY TOMMY THOMPSON

How I Lost the Love of My Life and Became Wealthy as a Result

How I Used The Law of Attraction to Unlock Health, Wealth, And Happiness

TOMMY THOMPSON

StoryTerrace

Design Mitar Stjepcevic, on behalf of StoryTerrace

Copyright © Tommy Thompson and StoryTerrace

Text is private and confidential

First print August 2022

StoryTerrace

www.StoryTerrace.com

CONTENTS

SECTION 1	9
SECTION 2	23
SECTION 3	31
SECTION 4	43
SECTION 5	59
SECTION 6	67
SECTION 7	77
SECTION 8	85
DEDICATIONS	97

I used to tell people I had a very boring life with moments of extreme excitement—like stuff that nobody should have to experience kind of thing, right?

SECTION 1

The Second Fire That Broke the Camel's Back

I was driving through town when I got a phone call from Ann. She said, "There's smoke coming out of the roof of the shop." And I said, "What do you mean there's smoke coming out of the roof of the shop? Is it coming out of the back where the exhaust is for the motor? Where's it coming out of?" And she said, "No, it's coming out of the peaks on either side of the shop."

At that time, she was home by herself with the dogs, so I literally started doing 160 kilometers per hour all the way back to get her out of that place because I knew exactly what was going on. I was probably about 25 minutes away, but by breaking all the traffic laws I could possibly break, it took me about 10 minutes to get home.

When I ran up to the house, Ann was frantic and shaking. She had already been back and forth to the shop herself to see what was going on because she wanted to try to save herself, to save us. I'm calm in these types of situations, but she's always panicked. After what happened with BC Hydro, she was always in a state of fear because it was a generator job and there was helicopter traffic going all the time.

I told Ann to get everything that was important to her once again: Get the dogs, get everything that was valuable, everything that meant anything to her. I told her, "Just go! Get the hell out of here!" We didn't have anywhere to necessarily go, but she loaded up the truck with whatever she possibly could and left me there. I headed back into the shop to try to figure out what was going on.

It was pretty much all on fire.

When I got into the building, I could hear the crackling. I could hear what was going on plus the sound of the generator, which was quite loud all the time.

I went through the hallways and into the back generator room and turned off the fuel source to the generator right away. I knew the building was on fire, yet with the generator still going, there was a chance of things becoming much, much worse. I needed to get that motor. I cut the fuel source, and then I started to seek out where the fire was.

The building had two levels, so now, I was running around, trying to grab my water hoses and stuff that I used for watering, things like that. And I had a saw in my hand, plus a sledgehammer, and I was trying to bust through walls and find where this fire was to see if I could somehow put it out before the damage went too far.

I went into one room. I chopped apart the ceiling and got the hose up, spraying inside the ceiling. I could feel the water rolling back on me. It was scalding hot. I could hear the crackling—I knew the fire was right there. I could feel the heat. There was more and more and more smoke, and I realized, *OK, I must be at the wrong spot*. So, I dragged my hose a little bit further down. I kept progressing, but I couldn't see anything because it was getting too smoky.

I went into the next room, and that's where I saw the ceiling was wide open. The room was fully engulfed in flames, so I ran back to grab my hose. I was pulling my hose toward the fire so I could spray it and try to put it out . . . and I ran out of hose about 15 feet away from the fire.

It was almost like a cartoon. I remember actually saying that to myself with kind of a chuckle in the back of my mind before thinking, *I'm not going to let myself die in this scenario*.

Instead, I thought, *OK, well, I'm done here now. I've done all I can possibly do as a person who's already taken way too many chances*, and I started running back downstairs.

Now at the time, we had just had a harvest, so we had probably $30,000 to $40,000 worth of product hanging—probably even more than that. I opened the door, and I saw this. Obviously, the fire was getting worse and worse; on the whole upper floor, things were starting to fall down. The lights were flickering and going out because the electrical was being affected. Once the lights started to flicker and stuff like that, I got a little bit more nervous.

But then I looked up, and I saw all the product hanging there, and I started to feel like I had to try and save something.

So I ran downstairs, and instead of getting the hell out of there, I started ripping product down and bagging it in garbage bags. I think I grabbed four or five bags—all I could basically carry—and I headed out of the shop the back way through the bush. I threw the bags over the fence, climbed it, and went through the ravine and up through the bush, dragging these bags of product.

I ended up on the side of the road in a ditch, hiding, waiting for either Ann or another gentleman whom we had already contacted who knew what was going on. I lay there watching vehicles pass, waiting for the right one to drive by to come and get me.

The whole time, I could hear the fire trucks on the way. The whole building was on fire. It was in the papers. It was on the news.

Almost everything Ann and I had was gone. Again. It was the fire that broke the camel's back, and nothing would ever be the same.

We had been together 21 years. Ann was the love of my life. If she would have said something to me, I would have moved mountains to change whatever needed to be changed.

It Was the Best of Places; It Was the Worst of Places

I used to say to Ann that we were in the best and the worst place that we'd been in for a long time. We were both working great jobs, yet we were still stuck in a crappy kind of living situation. But I'd tell her, "That's not gonna last. Even though we're in this shithole, it's only temporary."

How we ended up in the trailer is we went to my boss's house with all that stuff right after the fire. He was a great guy, and he said, "I got nowhere for you guys to go. However, I've got this place. It's not a very desirable place to live, but you can stay there as long as you like, free of cost. You just have to pay for your own cable."

The property was gorgeous. It had a beautiful creek running through it, and it was quiet and lovely. But the trailer off to the side in the bush along the creek was left empty for many, many years. It was moldy. It was grungy; it was leaky; it was damp. It was horrible!

We had heat, but if you turned that heat on, the hydro bill was through the roof. I didn't have to pay the bill, but if I cranked the heat up all the time, I would get a phone call saying, "How come the bloody hydro bill is through the roof? Turn the heat off. That's what you have a fireplace for." So, I would have to burn wood regularly to keep that place warm, which was a bit of a hassle, especially when both of us were working full-time jobs, with two big dogs living with us as well.

But the boss liked me there because it slowed down the break-ins that kept happening when it was unattended, making it look like nobody lived on the property. With two big dogs, that was kind of a bonus for him.

But it didn't make Ann feel any better.

What Color Do You Like Your Water?

You could call that area Iron Mountain because the content in the water was absolutely ridiculous. Now, they had an osmosis and a water treatment system for the property, but it never worked. That meant the water was orange—and not a nice orange but like an unpleasant orange. Unless you like that in your clothes, then it's not as good as you might think.

For all of the clothes that mattered—work clothes in particular— Ann had to use the laundromat 30 minutes away. So, she had all these white dress shirts that she hated wearing already, but to keep them white, they all went to the laundromat. Ironically, it burned down over one weekend, and she had no shirts for the next week. Then we had to go significantly further away for clean clothes that weren't orange.

Ann was definitely a natural beauty, but she also loved her things. She was a girly girl, no question about it. Always. You know, she wouldn't leave the house without looking the way she needed to look. She could do a ponytail with a baseball cap but from basically the forehead down had to be pristine before she left the house.

We had filtered water that we drank, obviously. I would warm up some filtered water in the kettle, then mix cold and warm water in a jug and use that so she could shampoo her hair in the morning before she went to work. Which sometimes, when we both had early starts, was a bit of a pain in the butt kind of thing, right? But it was one of those things that we did because we had to, and it was temporary—but looking back, it obviously bothered her a great deal.

It wasn't what Ann was used to. It wasn't what she had signed up for 21 years before.

Whereas me, I tried to look at it as just something that we needed to do right now, so we should just do it and not dwell on the negative aspects of it. Instead, we could have a laugh kind of thing, right? But having that mentality hasn't always been my saving grace. If somebody tells me they're having a bad day, and I say, "Don't worry, there's another one coming"—that's not actually helpful.

So, we were living in that situation, and I tried to keep my head at *Yeah, this sucks, but it's gonna get us there. Yes, we're here now, but we're not gonna stay here. This is just a stepping stone we have to deal with to get where we want to be.* That sort of thing. And while I knew Ann was unhappy and getting angrier and angrier because she didn't like her job, that was my attitude: It's just temporary. But I look back now, and I don't think she got the empathy and the sympathy that she needed from me.

Because of my background in personal training and nutrition, sometimes people wanted information from me. Some of the things I took very seriously, and some things I would joke about. I'd say something to someone, and Ann would look at me and say, "Why would you say something like that?" And I'd say, "What? I'm just being honest. I'm trying to help them. I'm being nice!" She'd say, "Yeah, you're nice, but you're a hard nice. That doesn't go over very well." And it certainly didn't go over very well with Ann in that trailer.

Yet, I thought I was doing all the right things. In my mind, I was still lifting her up, putting her on that pedestal because she deserved the best.

The Nicest House With the Best Bears

The job site where the second fire took place was called The Forest. It was three levels, probably 4,000 square feet. We had a large bedroom with a full en suite plus two other full-size bedrooms and a family room on the top floor that I used for cardio and yoga.

On the main floor was our living area, which was gorgeous. It had a nice office, a big kitchen, a big dining area and, off the side of the house, a swimming pool that was quite nice. It was all landscaped and surrounded by greenbelt, so we had deer and lots of bears and wildlife all the time.

Ann used to feed the blue scrubs and the squirrels right out of her hand. She fed the birds and the deer so often that the bears used to actually sleep in her flower garden. We would get up in the morning in the summertime, and she would look out and go, "Yep, sure enough, he's there." She'd walk out and literally be five feet away from the bear, clap her hands and be like, "OK big boy, time to go." And it would get up and wander off into the bush, right?

It was paradise for Ann. It was paradise for both of us.

It was the opposite of the trailer. The trailer was hell.

The Greenhouse That Wouldn't Come Back

I couldn't give her that house back, but I did try to give her something else to make her happy again.

At The Forest, Ann had had her own garden. Her dad had bought her a greenhouse that we ended up losing, which was another heartbreak for her because it had been a gift, and she was very, very close with her dad.

I had to keep going back to try to save that thing because she was so upset that she was leaving the greenhouse that her dad got her, and I ended up with it all in pieces. Well, those things—when they're taken apart like that, they just don't go back together the same kind of way.

I tried to rebuild it when we were at the trailer so she'd have that bit of a sanctuary, something that she could do outside of stressing out about living in that crap hole. A nice little garden that she could go to and get out of her head for a little while—but she couldn't, because, of course, I couldn't rebuild it. The ground wasn't level. I was on my own, and I didn't know what I was doing.

I was trying to appease her, trying to do whatever I could. I hated going back in the trailer every time I tried to start building the greenhouse. I hated going in there and telling her, "Baby, I just can't get this thing together. It's not working."

I knew I had already hurt her so bad with everything that was going on, and it broke my heart seeing her having to live like that, right? She was my princess. Even though she may not have felt like that at the end, that's how I still feel about it now.

We Had a Three-Year Plan

It was very unpleasant, and we were kind of trapped there. We had two large dogs, so it wasn't very easy to rent a place, but my job was fantastic, and her job was doing really, really well, even though she hated it. So we had a three-year plan to get ourselves out.

Ann was unhappy. She wasn't very friendly. But we were both unhappy because of what we were dealing with, so I thought it was a shared emotion, not a one-sided emotion, if you know what I mean.

I even said to her one time when she was complaining about her job, "Don't worry, honey, because by the time we're ready to get out of here, I'll be high enough on the seniority list that you will be able to leave. Just put a couple more years in, and you can retire early." She looked at me and said, "Are you serious?" I said, "Of course I'm serious."

Of course, maybe I did have those feelings to a certain degree about not liking how she was feeling and not knowing how to make it better.

But in my mind, I thought we were both experiencing the same thing; the only difference was she was thinking about it differently. She was looking at what she was dealing with instead of looking at where we were going, whereas I was trying to ignore what we were experiencing and only see where we were going.

I didn't understand that that made all the difference in the world to Ann.

About a year and a half into that three-year plan is when she walked out the door. It was like she dropped the ball in the middle of the game and walked off the field.

SECTION 2

It Was Like Any Other Day

Ann was the love of my life. We had been together 21 years, and I expected to be with her forever. I didn't see it coming.

At all.

I came home from work one afternoon, and Ann was sitting on the couch. She got up, walked down the hall, then came back in. As I was going to get my hug, she looked at me with a kind of look in her eye and just said, "I can't do it anymore. I'm not happy. I have to leave. I feel like I'm losing my light."

I was completely dumbfounded. I couldn't understand what the heck was going on. I said, "How do you expect to be able to afford this? What are you going to do? How are you going to eat?"

Ann said, "I don't want any of your money." Then she literally refused to talk about it any longer.

That was all she had to say.

The Christmas Cap

A few months before Ann left, she said, "Don't spend a lot on me at Christmas this year." She set a limit on what we each should spend. I thought it was coming from a wanting-to-save-money perspective; afterward, I realized it was because she was already planning to leave.

So when Christmas rolled around, I had bought her a nice winter coat and several items that equaled the amount we set. But in the pocket of the coat that I bought her was a $2,500 wedding band to go with her wedding set, and there was a beautiful chain and diamond earrings in the other pocket.

I said, "Make sure you check your pockets!" She pulled out the extra presents that I'd bought with the money she told me I wasn't allowed to spend. The way I looked at it, I finally had a job making over 100 grand a year. I wanted to spoil my girl and give her everything she wanted.

Ann looked happy and upset at the same time. You could tell that her heart was broken a little bit because I spent that money, and I think that her heart was broken a little bit because she was planning to leave, and I'm not the type of person to take things back. I think taking those gifts put a lot of guilt on her.

But it wasn't enough to change her mind.

At First, She Told Me Nothing

So after weeks of mostly silence, I helped Ann move out. I helped her with everything. I had spent 21 years taking care of this woman, so I couldn't in good conscience not help her, even when she would barely talk to me. Even having just regular conversations, you know when you're in a room with a person who doesn't really want to be around you. That was how it was with Ann.

Later, it was the same. In the beginning, when I was just trying to get her sorted, I would be there—not all the time, but a lot of times. I would drop things off from Costco and say, "Hi," and see how she was doing. I would always try to have a happy kind of attitude, but I could tell—she couldn't stand me being there.

I especially remember when I first went over, and she had her place all set up. I looked around and went, "Wow. There's literally no me anywhere!" I got the feeling she couldn't wait for me to leave.

At one point, I said to Ann, "You know, after 21 years, I deserve some explanation of why this is taking place." Because at first, she told me nothing. Finally, she said to me that it was 80% our lifestyle choice and 20% the things that aggravate every other couple. That's the only explanation I've ever received from her.

After 21 years.

You're Not Wearing Your Ring

At first, Ann said to me, "I need time and space." And I thought, *OK, well, maybe she just needs to be out of here.*

Early on in the relationship, when we were in that sort of criminal element, I had told her, "I'm happy if you live somewhere else, and I'll take care of business. Then, we'll just spend weekends together." When she said that she needed space, I was still wearing my ring, and Ann was still wearing hers, so I guess there was a part of me that thought, *Well, let her take her time and space and do what she needs. I'll just keep plugging along, and we'll be OK.*

Then one day, I saw Ann and I noticed the ring was gone. That hit me like a punch in the stomach. I said to her, "You're not wearing your ring anymore," and she started going, "Well, blah blah blah . . . " I said, "That's OK. That's fine." I still wore my ring for a couple more weeks, and then I finally decided it was time for me to take mine off, too.

And then I sat down with Ann, and I told her, "Never mind the time and space; my ring is coming off. This is obviously what you want, so, you know, I wish the best for you, and I'm going to do everything I can to help you."

And that was it.

It Wasn't Her Fault

When I met Ann, she was six feet tall, but she was a bit heavy, mostly because of the drinking and the smoking and the bad diet kind of thing. Her favorite candy was the Skor bar, so I would sneak them all over the place for her. When she came to work and opened up her till, there would be one sitting there; I would sneak one into her pocket when she was busy, and when she'd go grab her keys, there would be a Skor bar hanging out there. I guess I've always liked putting surprises in her pockets.

I can't fault Ann for doing something that she felt she had to do. I always tell people, "Don't stay in a situation that doesn't make you happy."

I mean, I knew she was unhappy, but I was making light of our situation because I knew that it was a means to an end. I didn't see how heavily it was weighing on her. I had so much on my plate, and I was putting so much time in at work, and my dog was ill. I didn't catch it until it was too late. For me, everything was going according to the way things were supposed to be going. Like I said, I thought her unhappiness was a shared feeling.

Not a one-sided unhappiness.

I told her when she decided to leave, "You know, you basically made yourself hate me. You put yourself in a situation where you analyzed everything that was wrong about me and didn't look at what was good, and you made yourself hate me. That's how you could push me away the way you did. But if you would have at least said something, I would have moved mountains to get us out of this situation if I knew that this is what it was doing to our relationship."

It was too late. That's when Ann walked out.

That's when I found out this was obviously a one-sided unhappiness because she was literally willing to throw away 21 years of what many people who knew us probably considered one of the best relationships they had ever seen. I thought we were a shining example of a couple who gets through life without the normal issues that everybody else deals with.

There was never any fighting or arguing. Of course, we had disagreements, but there was no screaming, no ranting and throwing things, no walking out on each other. There was never any of that type of behavior in our relationship. No cheating.

No warning.

Unless you looked way back, before Ann and I ever met.

The Mean Streets of Montreal Versus the Jehovah's Witnesses

My stepfather, the man who raised me, was British. He was a very smart man, very highly educated, but he loved having his fingers in bad things, you know what I mean? He loved having that little bit of darkness in his life. I don't know why; it was just his way. For example, the house that he built on 54 Legion Street in St. Hubert was built primarily with stolen equipment and stolen materials.

He associated with a lot of bikers, like the Popeyes, who were a very popular motorcycle gang back in the day, and Satan's Choice. I'm not sure how, but he befriended these guys and used to do things for them, like load up the trunk of his '68 Pontiac Strato Chief with weapons and drive them across the border into New York so the Popeyes could have their rumbles. When they were done, they would call my stepfather, and he'd come, load the weapons back in, and drive home. Because he was British, very well read, and well spoken, he never got stopped.

So, I grew up comfortable with cops knocking on the door and rough elements around. I grew up witnessing violence.

One time, my brother was badly beaten by seven guys, right on the main drag. He had crawled across the street to get away from these guys, and in Montreal, every gas station was a Fiat dealership, right? They were all linked together. So, he went to the dealership on the corner of our street, but the guy locked the door. My brother was covered in blood and was left for dead.

Well, once my uncle realized what had happened, he ended up burning that place right to the ground because they didn't help my brother. Then, my father and his biker buddies went after each and every individual in a very bad way, to retaliate.

That's how it was where I came from.

On the other hand, Ann grew up in a Jehovah's Witness household where she was not allowed to have her own feelings, so even though she was a bright light—very loving, compassionate, and emotional—she was also insecure and avoided confrontations.

I mean, she would talk to me and get things off her chest, but I think she kept her deepest emotions about our relationship to herself. She wasn't hiding her feelings so much as staying away from anything that would cause a fight. She would never sit down and communicate, really hammer out the problems of trying to get through this lifestyle and make sure we got to wherever it was that we needed to go, kind of thing. That led me to believe there were no real issues.

But Ann had issues, and she was scared all the time. She just never told me. Instead, at the end, she developed and nurtured a resentment, an anger, toward me because of the circumstances we were in, rather than realizing this was a shared, not one-sided, situation.

Ann made herself hate me so she could leave.

SECTION 3

I saw Ann for the first time out of the corner of my eye. Six feet tall, blonde haired, blue eyed . . . absolutely stunning. Just, you know, a beacon of light. You could see that glow around her all the time, and the energy she gave off was just fantastic. I never actually spoke to her at that time, but I certainly did notice her.

How I Got From the Gym to the Bar

Bodybuilding was vital for me my whole life, even in my youngest years. I started as a competitive bodybuilder when I was 17; I was extremely good at it, and I just loved it.

I don't know what it was that I loved about it. Maybe it was simply because I was one of those classic stories: A sickly, small kid who started to work out and "got bit by the iron bug," as they say. My brother bought me the Arnold Schwarzenegger weight set for Christmas when I was 13 years old, and that was it.

That's how I ended up owning a gym, which was a lifelong dream of mine. But it wasn't until my business partners/ex-in-laws kicked me out and changed the alarm code that I got to the place where I met Ann.

First, I spent a couple of nights in the park sleeping on a bench, waiting for my flight attendant girlfriend, Jane, to get back from Japan. I met her at her door, basically, and ended up living with her as I wasn't actually doing anything else at the time. I was homeless, and the people who came to my aid were my friends in the industry. It was then I started to seek out opportunities and found people who said: "OK, we need a guy. We can set you up in a house to do this." And that's how it all sort of started. It wasn't a plan. It just happened that way.

I've always been an optimist. I was always moving forward. So even though it wasn't necessarily where I should have been, I was still doing my best and trying to make as much money as I could.

Through that connection, I actually met a friend who trained at the same gym as I did and had investments in the industry. We started talking about needing a good part-time job because, I mean, it's great to make that kind of money from a house, but you need to be able to do something on paper as well, right?

So, we were bullshitting that one day, and he suggested the bar because it was an ideal job. It took place at night, and the pay wasn't too bad - though when you thought about how much work it was, it was terrible. But, you know, it was money coming in, and it allowed a lot of freedom for training. He said, "Come by. Check it out. It's an easy gig. Throw out some drunks and hang out all night."

So I went, and I was standing there, talking to him, when I saw Ann that first time.

In the Beginning of Us

I came back and got hired, and when I was introduced to Ann, she looked at me and said, "Oh, finally, they're hiring some good-looking doormen." And I'm a bit of a jokester, so of course, I looked over my shoulder and said, "Who is she talking about? I don't see any." And pretty much from that moment, we were kind of flirty and talked a lot and got close. And, you know, it sort of went from there.

I was drawn to her. I think everybody was drawn to her. She was such a bright light.

The first six months, I spent most of my time hanging out with Ann. She had a fantastic sense of humor and was extremely social, with such an energy about her. I was always very impressed by how hard she worked and how much she did, so I would help her with as much as I could. Basically, the first six months, we were courting.

Because of the nature of my job, I had lots of free time on my hands, so I would meet Ann in the morning at the bar and cut up limes and lemons for her, get the beer kegs—whatever menial job that she would normally do herself. That's how our relationship started off, with all the wonderful little niceties that my mama taught me.

But you know, she drank way too much, mostly encouraged by the industry that she was in. She would be at work until three or four in the morning, cashing out the waitresses and all the other bartenders, dealing with the money, and doing all that stuff. She'd close the bar down, so she'd be there till four in the morning, and normally by that stage, she'd just be hammered. Then, she would walk home, get up in the morning, and be back at the bar by 11.30 a.m., setting up, prepping, and getting everything ready. Then, she'd go home, get dressed, come back and do it all again. When I say she was drinking, Ann did this all while being frickin' hammered and hung over 95% of the time, and she did it brilliantly.

I remember when we first started to see each other, I used to remove myself from the door so I could be there by the bar for her. She would be so drunk. She would come up and lean on me, and she'd go, "Oh my god, I'm so hammered. I gotta get out of here." Then, a group of people would walk up to the bar, and she would snap out of it, take all the drink orders, and take everybody's money at the same time. *Bang, bang, bang, bang*—knock off every drink. *Bang, bang, bang, bang*—knock off everybody's cash. Walk away, lean back over to me, and go, "Oh my god, I'm so drunk. I can barely stand up."

But it was easy to overlook this because of the type of person that she was. Ann had just such an energy about her. I think that's one of the things that broke my heart the most when she told me that she felt like she was losing her light when she left me. That really, really messed me up because I felt like I was actually partially responsible for giving her that light in the first place by taking her out of the environment that was slowly killing her.

With This Ring

I remember when Ann told me I was her first serious boyfriend.

She had a nice silver band that she wore on her index finger. I was holding her hands at the bar one night—we were having kind of an intimate moment—and I slid it off her finger and slipped it on my wedding finger.

She looked at me, and her eyes welled up, and she said, "What are you doing?" And I said, "I'm putting your ring on my finger to make sure that you understand how I feel about you. So that you can feel secure."

*

Ann and I continued to get closer, and people recognized there was a relationship developing between us because I was always helping around the bar, and we were always together. Other people could see that.

One of the things Ann used to do before I started at the bar was stay late and play pool tournaments after work. I had offered to drive her home, and she said, "Oh, no, that's fine. I'll walk." But I found out she walked through a grubby bush in a bad part of town, and I thought, *Oh my god—I can't believe you're walking through there at three in the morning!* So, I also ended up driving her home on a nightly basis. That's how we got to know each other. That's how we courted.

At the time, I was living with Jane and driving Ann home in Jane's vehicle because Ann and I were still just friends.

I joked with her because she would always kiss everybody good night, but when I would drop her off at home, she'd say, "Later," and I would wait till she got in the building, and then I would leave. One night, I said to her, "How can you kiss everybody else good night, but you don't kiss me?" And she gave me a little smirk and walked away.

So, we both knew we weren't going to stay just friends for long. And we didn't.

I Made a Decision That Lasted 21 Years

We were boyfriend and girlfriend, and I'd been staying with Ann in her little apartment in New West when she ended up contracting both strep throat and mono, though we didn't know that at the time. She just got very sick.

I would come home every night, put her in an alcohol bath to bring her temperature down, and put her back to sleep. In the morning, she'd still be sick but somewhat OK, but when I'd get home from the bar, her temperature was back up to 104. It was just a complete mess. On the fourth night, I said, "Honey that's it. Get in the shower. I don't know what you have to do but do it because I gotta take you to the hospital."

Ann didn't have to stay in the hospital, but they put a shunt in her arm, so she had to return, morning and evening, for five days. And during that time, I started the process of completely taking care of my princess. I had a big empty house just sitting there in Birdland, and I said, "OK. That's it."

I told Ann I quit her job for her and mine too, and then I moved her entire house by myself into my pickup truck. At the end, she was lying on her loveseat, so I carried her down and threw the loveseat in the back, and that was the last we ever saw of that place. I moved her into my house, and she was living with me. She had no job, so she was my dependent. She didn't get a lot of time to think about it; I just started paying her bills and being somebody she could rely on, kind of thing. Ann had no say in the matter, no time to think about it. There was no discussion.

And that was that.

My end game had always been to make as much money as I possibly could to give Ann the life she deserved. I wanted to give her everything she could possibly want and, at the same time, get the same for myself and, obviously, move toward early retirement. The possibilities were great as long as everything went well. Unfortunately, nothing ever goes perfectly in that type of industry.

I remember when Ann left me, she drove away in her truck—a vehicle that I bought her. I was trying to explain some of the technology to her, and she said to me, "I know, I know, I KNOW!" I said, "Well, I'm sorry. I've been taking care of you for 21 years, so it's a little hard for me just to stop."

Here's a funny thing, though, that ties the beginning of our love story to the end:

I was still in a rebound relationship with Jane, but she knew we were coming to an end. When I left her for Ann, she said to me,

"You're never going to have a good relationship in your life because you've never lived on your own, and you've never been your own person. So, you can continue to go on the way you're going, but you will never have a successful relationship."

And when Ann said to me, "I can't do this anymore," the first thing that popped into my head was what Jane had said, and I thought, *Wow, you were right.*

SECTION 4

"They're Here"

We had been in this place for almost six years when we heard the rumors about BC Hydro trying to figure out a way to shut down grow ops. One of their techniques was getting together with the fire department and the police and using public safety as a way to get into people's houses without a warrant. If your house was using excessive amounts of hydro, you would basically go on a list.

Well, one morning, we were having coffee and actually talking about that very subject. Then Ann looked over at me and said,

"They're here."

I said, "What do you mean 'they're here'?"

And she got up really quickly, looked toward the window, and said again,

"THEY'RE HERE."

I looked out through the blinds, and I could see the fire truck and the police cars surrounding the house.

So, Ann, the dog, and I scurried off to the bedroom to hide out. We tucked ourselves away in a little area where we could be hidden as they banged and shouted, wandering around the house, making a complete ruckus, trying to get us to come to the door. They were baiting us with almost crazy behavior.

We didn't come out.

When it finally settled down, we waited quite a while before we left our hiding spot. Then, we went out and checked, and sure enough, there was a notice pinned to the door. We had 48 hours to arrange an appointment so BC Hydro could come in and check out the problem with the power because the house was drawing far too much for a single-family dwelling.

I promptly contacted them to make the arrangements for the inspection. We then got a crew to come in and get everything cleaned out. Drywall, flooring—everything was done within 48 hours. Then, we just waited for them to come.

That Saturday, I was at the Home Show, representing the construction company I worked for while Ann was home alone with the dog.

And they came again.

I got a frantic call while I was at the head of a long lineup, handing out brochures, greeting people with a smile, and talking about pine beetles, while on the other end of the phone, my girl was in a complete panic. She was frightened to death because the police were literally pounding on the door.

She was crying, "I think they're coming in! I think they're coming in!"

They were banging at the windows and kicking, doing all sorts of stuff trying to freak her out as she was crying on the phone to me. Five minutes of this went by, and then she said, "Oh my god, OK . . . everything's just gone black. Everything's gone quiet."

They had pulled the hydro meter off the side of the house.

What was Hydro's explanation for why they came back the way they did? They claimed I had given the wrong number to book the appointment. Of course, that wasn't true.

So, I came home, and she was obviously quite upset. I mean, we were both upset due to the circumstances. It was not a good situation.

We lost all the money that we had because we didn't control that aspect of it; the other guys controlled the money. So, there was no money for us to go anywhere. I actually hung on to five pounds of weed that technically they would consider me stealing to make sure that I could move that and have money to get a place. But that was where the problem was.

We couldn't just jump into another place because we had product, not money, and neither of us had actual real jobs. When you rent a place, they tend to want that information. It created a bit of a situation for us. We needed to get rid of that weed to have the money in our hands, and then I had to convince the next landlord to let us move in as quickly as we possibly could.

We ended up living in that house for three or four more months through the winter—the coldest months—with no heat, no power, no nothing. We had to heat our food in the fireplace in the house and burn wood. We had to sleep in our winter clothing, and if we were going to be intimate, we had to remain completely dressed throughout that event.

That was probably one of the very first moments, you know, that scared the crap out of her. And I was not there. Soon afterward, we knew what we had to do: Live like the rest of the population and scrape to make ends meet while both of us worked.

Legally.

In the Beginning: The Outlaw Life

I brought Ann into this life, but she came along. Willingly. It's not like I dragged her into it and trapped her.

She was drinking too much on the job, paying her alcohol tab with her tips. She wasn't in a place she should be, spiritually, mentally, or physically. Then, she found someone who put her on a pedestal and took care of her, something she'd never had with another guy. So, for her, in the beginning, I think it was absolutely fantastic.

She was very happy when she didn't have to go to work and could sleep in every day. She was a princess. She always had money in her pocket. She had her nails and hair done whenever she wanted. She had the freedom to do what she wanted.

There was also a certain degree of intrigue with the industry. It's always kind of fun to be on that end of it, you know, to have that experience.

Like when I got paid—and we were always paid in cash—I would come home and put money on the pillow beside her head. She would be asleep still until noon, but when she would wake up, she'd be smiling with a 10 pack next to her face. I used to say, "That's a wonderful way to wake up, with $10,000 staring back at you."

She lived a princess lifestyle, and she loved it. If you can have that kind of experience and not get yourself in deep trouble, that's even better.

Ann still had fears back then, but they were different fears, smaller. We were on smaller jobs with my partner, and I would be doing a lot of the legwork myself—I'd do runs and carry stuff, do deliveries, stuff like that. But even then, she would always be worried about me getting hurt because I was working alone. I was dealing with the underbelly of society, so every single time I'd go meet some strange person for whatever reason, I had to remember that I wasn't meeting the best of people. Ultimately, being part of that, I realized I was the underbelly, too.

In an outlaw life, there is always something going to go wrong, and there's no one to call.

If someone breaks into your house and rips off your grow op, you can't rely on the police. It doesn't work that way. It's basically fight or flight. Obviously, the smartest thing to do is say, "Yes, sir. Yes, sir. Take whatever you need, and be on your way, sir." And hopefully nobody gets hurt, though a lot of times it doesn't pan out that way. An outlaw life means being comfortable with cops knocking on the door or having that element in the house all the time and being in that sort of environment on a regular basis.

With this lifestyle, you've got to understand things can go wrong and not let those things define or control your choices. If I get caught, I'm not going to be frantic and try to run. I've heard the stories of guys running through the bush in their underwear—well, that's not me. If I'm in underwear, I'm caught. I'm calling my lawyer because I am not running around in my underwear. I have dignity.

And that was not Ann. She had no idea how to live like that.

Nor did Ann have any idea what my partner was like. He's probably in jail right now. He was a very, very bad guy. I'm not even gonna mention his name or anything because he was a very scary character. I mean, we got along fine, but I was used to being around those types of people. I knew the things not to say or do and the things that I could get away with saying or doing.

He was always nice to Ann and everything, and if you were to meet him on the street, you'd think he was a nice guy. But if you knew him from where I knew him from—this was a person who would cut your head off in a heartbeat and not even lose a minute of sleep about it. He was hard. You could see it. You could feel that energy. He was a little fellow, but he was a little fellow I would be hard-pressed to ever cross.

He told me a story one time when I went over to his house to pick up my paycheck. He had a lot of weapons out, and he was telling me somebody had just ripped them off, and he was going to meet them. I said, "What do you need? Do you need back up?"

He pulled open his jacket to show me he had two hand grenades hanging inside.

He said, "No. I go myself to these meetings, and the first thing I do is I put one of these on the table. If anybody wants to cause any problems, not only am I going, everybody's going."

I was like, "OK, I'll be on my way now."

He was a very, very frightening individual, but from the way he interacted with Ann, you would think he was a wonderful, wonderful guy. You wouldn't even for a second see anything bad in him. Ann didn't. But she was still always worried, always a little bit afraid, right from the start.

There and Back Again

After the BC Hydro thing, I was living with Ann in a really nasty, bug-infested place in Whalley because they accepted our dogs. She was at Costco, and I was, you know, working a job, just like everybody else. I was the same mouse on the wheel.

I remember one day, I was cleaning bathrooms in a gym that I worked at, and a friend of mine who was a fellow competitor came in and saw me cleaning toilets. He said, "What the hell are you doing?" And I said, "Well, I'm cleaning toilets."

I was actually a personal trainer, but when something needed to be done, I just did it. It wasn't like I was the guy that was designated to clean the toilets, but I didn't have a problem with cleaning the toilets if the toilets needed cleaning, kind of thing. And that's where my friend confronted me and said, "You are so much better than that."

He wanted to introduce me to some guys because of how hard I worked and how dedicated I was to all the things I did; he thought that I would be perfect for this particular job. That's how I got introduced to the bigger end of the industry. As frightening as my ex-partner was, these guys were on a much grander scale in every way. We could go from making 8–10k solo to 25–30k.

Per month.

And that's when I kind of decided, *OK, well here's somewhere I could go*, even though I had promised Ann that I would never bring her down that road again. We were at a point of normalcy where we were living like everybody else. We had decided together that we were going to make it like everybody else. But we were struggling. Like everybody else.

That's why, when the introduction to these guys was proposed to me, I presented it to her as an opportunity to work in the same business but on a much larger level, with a much larger, consistent payday, and without any work necessarily on the outside. I would have only one job, which was to run the show.

It was like: *We don't really want to do this, but the money is so much that it's hard to say no*. And when I told Ann how much money we could be making, she was obviously very interested and went along with me. Honestly, I'm pretty sure I sold her on the idea partially with the fact that it was a generator job, so it greatly reduced certain risks. But of course, it increased other risks.

After that, Ann was always nervous. There was a lot of helicopter traffic all the time because it was that kind of job, and every time one flew over the house or somebody we didn't know rang the doorbell or was at our gate, she would panic; she always felt like she was being watched. But we couldn't say no to the money.

And that's how we got back in.

They Call it Being on Lockdown

So for the next 12 years, we did take it to the next level, with a much bigger payday and much more potential. That meant living on the job site 24/7. They call it "being on lockdown." You have no close friends, no confidantes, few family functions. And this was one of the things that was very, very difficult for Ann because, obviously, you live your life as a lie.

Ann was a very social person. She played pool tournaments. She loved hanging out with friends, going out for drinks, all of that, while I did not because I had been an athlete all my life. That party type of lifestyle didn't necessarily appeal to me very much, but the only time we got to do that type of stuff anyway was when our own group was going out and we could be involved in that type of event.

We couldn't just go anywhere and talk to anybody and have that freedom. We just couldn't.

Which for me, because I was living that victim mentality where it was the world against me, was fine. I never had a problem with not being around people because I was never overly fond of them. Also, because of my background and how I was raised in that element, it wasn't an uncomfortable environment for me. That's not to say that it was right or wrong. It's just to say that it didn't have the same effect on me emotionally as it did on Ann, who was in a constant state of anxiety.

Unfortunately, I did not see that. And she did not express that.

Ann put up a pretty good front; she was a very strong woman that way. But it was just a front, and she was very delicate on the inside. For the longest time, I felt we were on the same page, and I always felt I was protecting her in certain circumstances, but my mental perspective of the whole situation was obviously much different from hers.

I can see that now. I did not see that then.

So, we were isolated. We did have some very, very close friends whom we could talk to from time to time, but still, it was very difficult. We had to hold back certain things just in case because you never knew who they might have told.

For Ann, I think that was almost worse than not having anyone at all.

A Gathering of the Usual Suspects

OK, we couldn't do all the normal things with our real friends and our real family. But we did have social functions within the industry that were lavish and also very uncomfortable. We used to call them gatherings of the usual suspects.

Mostly, they were concerts and events that took place in private boxes. Various celebrities would be at tables with certain very influential people in organized crime. "Influential" is a good word to describe them, though in that environment they didn't appear that way. We actually had guys that specifically wouldn't go because they were concerned about being photographed with other people who were there.

Even though we did do these things, it was just weird because of the situation. We were sort of all in the same world—we were acquaintances, and we could sort of talk freely together. But even though I might stand next to, say, one of the leaders of one of the chapters of the Hells Angels, having a laugh and a chuckle, and even if I'd seen them before at the bar or the gym, there was a sense of extreme uncomfortableness being with these types of people. No one could actually talk freely and be open in that environment.

I'll tell you a story. One of the guys that used to come to my gym was one of the very heavy hitters; he was actually a sergeant at arms for the Hells Angels. One day he goes, "You know, Tom, I was sitting at the bar one time, and I said to the girl next to me, 'Hey honey, pass me those peanuts.' And she's looking at me, and she goes, 'I'm not your fucking honey.' So I did the only thing I could do. I went and knocked out her boyfriend. When he came to, I looked at him and said, 'If your woman disrespects me one more time, I'm gonna hit you again.'"

So, as much as it was almost like being with my own group, I still was not able to be comfortable. If I uttered the wrong word or said the wrong thing, I could find myself in a very bad situation that I maybe couldn't get myself out of.

The only way out was to take or give whatever punishment was about to take place. There was no governing body that was going to step in and go, "Hey, no, come on now, that's not the responsible thing to do!" That was not going to happen because in that type of world, that was not the way things got done.

With these types of people, when you were having a laugh and joking around, everything was all fine and good. But a soldier like myself—I was not one of them. I was not a boss. I was not in charge. I was not running anything. I was very lucky to be there. Because I was one of the soldiers, I got special treatment, but if I said the wrong thing to the wrong person, I was completely replaceable.

So, was I extremely tense when my beautiful woman was walking around a little bit liquored up among these types of people? Oh, yeah. It was very hard for me to relax and not always feel a heartbeat away from a violent event that I was either going to have to initiate or protect myself from at any moment with any person I was dealing with at any time.

And I found myself often in situations where the men that I was standing around with were the kind of men that, if they wanted to take my woman to another room, I would have had to say, "OK, see you when you're done." Or suffer.

So that went on for basically 12 years. Those were our friends, and that was our life in lockdown. And I didn't see what it was doing to Ann.

At all.

SECTION 5

There was another thing that I used to say all the time whenever Ann was upset with me for whatever reason (it was never usually too serious, at least in my mind). I used to always joke with her and say, "Don't worry, honey. One day I'll be worth leaving."

Post Bombshell

Once I was hit with it, I was plunged into darkness. I didn't know what was going on. I was in my 50s; I'd been in this relationship for 21 years—I thought I had it all figured out. I had this woman I intended to continue to put on a pedestal, giving her everything I possibly could for the rest of my days. And you know, I thought I was done. Right? You think you're settled, that everything's taken care of.

I wasn't a happy guy after Ann broke my heart.

*

Ann was very short-tempered and cold throughout the entire time we were going through that transition, getting her ready to leave, and trying to find a place for her. Every time I tried to offer solutions or help, I was shot down or cut down. Every time I suggested she move back into the condo we owned together, she got even angrier. She would make food for herself but not me. My lunches and my stuff became my concern, no longer hers. You know, Ann was doing all the things she needed to do within herself to make it easy for her to make this move.

Meanwhile, I tended to be kind of an upbeat kind of a jokester, always trying to put a bright light on things, but for a little while there, I wasn't doing very well. I remember I walked into my dispatch office, and my boss looked at me and said, "How you doing today, Tommy?" And I said, "Apparently, there's room for improvement." And he said, "That's kind of a strange response from you. That's not what we're used to hearing." And I said again, "Well, apparently, as of late, I've just discovered there is some room for improvement." Instead of getting to the emotional side of it, I made a joke about it because it was a safety mechanism for me.

It was a sad environment. And quiet. So I started to think about a lot of things.

In the beginning of our life together, Ann lived the domestic goddess type of lifestyle. She worked in the yard, did her little flowers and cooked, and did things that she liked. She got her nails done, got her hair done, you know. She quite liked it. I believe the first time she went back to work was quite a few years in, and she had said to me the only reason she wanted to go back was because I was the only one she ever spoke to, and her people skills were starting to fail. She always had her fears, but she also had all this.

Now, 21 years later, what really stuck in my mind was the fact that I had a really, really good job with significant promise. Soon, she could quit working again for good. For her to walk away from that type of security made me think, *OK, well, this has got to be serious for her.*

I started thinking about relationships as a whole and what people expect from each other.

Ann left me when there was no arguing, yelling, fighting, or cheating. Those elements were not in the relationship, and she still said, *I need to get away from this person, even though he provides me with the financial security that I need.* At her age, you know, in her 40s—at that stage 48 or some-odd years old—she walked away from that.

I had to look at it through her eyes. I had to say to myself, *Wow, whatever is going on inside of her has to be much bigger than anything I could even conceivably think about or rationalize in my head.* I couldn't see it. She literally could have just stayed with me, and we would have plugged along like 95% of people do in an unhappy environment, paying our bills and getting by. We'd be on that treadmill that everybody experiences.

And I would have never done any of the things I'm doing now.

I realized being sad wasn't helping, so that's when I started doing things for Ann that she would want. I would give her money whenever she needed anything, and I started paying her on a regular basis when she moved out. I would put money on her credit cards when I put money on mine. When I went to Costco, I would call her and say, "What do you need?"

All these things took a little bit of the edge off Ann when she was dealing with me, and it gave me a little bit more power with respect to how I dealt with her because I started to change how I was looking at things. I started to see how 21 years with me looked and felt to Ann—the cumulative damage and fear of an outlaw life.

The First Fire at The Love Site

It was Christmas Eve morning, and I was woken up about 5 a.m. by my two Dobermans. They were freaking out and upset, so I let them out the back door, and they rushed into the backyard. It was still dark out, and I couldn't see anything, so they had their little run, and I got them back into the house.

When we got up at 8:30, I let them out again, and they were upset again, and I said, "I wonder what they're freaking out about?"

Well, it was because the generator room was on fire.

I rushed out in my housecoat and slippers to our back building, which was separate from the rest of everything. I opened up the first door, and the roof kind of collapsed on me. I went to open the second door, but it basically crumbled when I pushed it, it was so burned. I didn't really get inside the generator room because right in front of it was the fuel source, like a geyser of fire.

I quickly ran to shut the fuel source off while Ann, in her housecoat and slippers, was unraveling and running the hose to the back building so we could start trying to put the fire out. She kept having to squish the hose to get the frozen water through the line.

While all this was taking place, I called the people I needed to call. Someone was sent to help me, and another person was situated as a lookout to watch for fire trucks and police cars; he would contact me so I would have x amount of time to exit if I needed to.

As we were trying to get the hose going, a friend showed up through the back bush: Big Country. That was his actual nickname. He was a really great guy, part of our crew but also a volunteer firefighter.

We started tearing things down. It was still on fire, but we were getting it. We got the hose going. We were managing to get things under control and knock things down, so I asked Ann to grab us some coffee.

Obviously, before that, I had told her to load up the truck and get everything ready to bolt if she needed to because we were in a kind of secluded area. We thought we might be able to put this out without anybody being the wiser. Unfortunately, that didn't quite take place. As I was sitting down on the trailer in the backyard with the cup of coffee Ann brought me, I got the call: "OK, they're on their way."

At that point, I told Ann to get into the truck and get to our condo, which was like a safe house for us. Big Country and I stayed back and fought the fire and waited until we saw two firefighters walking up the driveway. Of course, we went out and greeted them.

One said, "Looks like you have a bit of a problem here." I said, "Yeah, but we got it mostly under control." He said, "Well, we should probably bring the truck up anyways, just to make sure." I said, "You're the captain." And they both turned around and headed off. Thank God. We knew the situation we were in, and if one of them had stayed, we would have had to subdue him to get away.

Once they were both out of our sight, Big Country and I did a quick run through the house, then headed out the back, through the bush, over shrubs and bushes, through ditches and around trees to a back road where there was a pickup truck waiting for us. We leapt into the back and shut the tailgate and canopy, and the vehicle took off.

There was only one way in and one way out of this place, and right as we were leaving, we looked out the back window, watching all the RCMP race by. We managed to make it out unscathed in that respect.

We did have to hide out while everything blew over, but at that time, we were 30 or 40 grand ahead of the game. We were in our condo, and most of our bills and credit cards were all cleared up. We were on a good roll. Things were going pretty well for us, even after that first fire.

But it was also the first really big scare for Ann. After that, she just stayed scared.

I didn't realize by the second fire that Ann had had enough—of the life and of me. But I had a lot of time, after the breakup, to look at everything—and mostly myself—from Ann's point of view.

Finally.

And what I saw made me change my life.

Finally.

SECTION 6

Heist

There was a documentary on Netflix called *Heist* about a woman and her boyfriend, who robbed armored cars. He was relatively successful—not that it ended up well for him. It never usually does in this type of scenario. But what hit me a little bit hard was how she carried on even after he was no longer in the picture.

She lived her life with her young child under the assumed name with the assumed passport until the epiphany came to her when her son became legal age that he didn't even know her real name. That's when she realized she would have to turn herself in and confess to her participation in those crimes to be able to give her son a normal life.

Watching that documentary and hearing that girl's story, even though it was much more violent and scary than what we went through, made me think of Ann. Not OUR story, but hers. The fact that this girl was willing to do things she wouldn't have normally done in the name of standing by her man made me look at Ann's fears differently—you know, the constant fears that she experienced once she was with me, after I moved her into my place and brought her into that life. She didn't have much recourse to get out, either, even if she really, really wanted to. What I didn't see then was that when I thought she was completely on board with everything we were doing, she was possibly doing those things because she didn't have any other option or choice at the time.

I think in the beginning, Ann was still blinded by the love aspect of things. It was only much later, when that wore off, obviously, that everything changed for her—or maybe not changed but became clear. This was no longer the life she had chosen or had ever wanted to have. Because although we led a somewhat boring life, and it was nice to have that kind of money coming in and be able to sleep in every day, there was always the fear.

In the industry, we used to say, "It's not the cops you gotta worry about. It's the rippers." It's the guys that actually get paid to go out and seek grow ops and rip them off. I've had a couple of friends badly beaten and left for dead by rippers. That's what we called them, anyway. That's what they do. They would just look for you, and when they found you, they would come in, put a gun to your head, and basically make you help them rip you off.

That's how we lived for 21 years. And I had no problem with it, because it was how I grew up. It was part of the Life.

Heist made me realize that all the time I thought I had a partner—like, you know, the Bonnie and Clyde type of scenario, where we were both moving forward in pursuit of the same thing—really, it was me leading and Ann going along with me. She may not have liked it, but she still participated in all of the activities when I needed her help, making plant babies or moving stuff or working because my crew wasn't available for whatever reason. She was always there, always watching, noticing everything; we called her the watchdog. Honestly, that was probably why she was under so much stress so often. She was never not watching. Or feeling like she was being watched.

Again, I didn't force her into that situation, but it's not like we ever had a long conversation about the impact and results and possible outcomes of that lifestyle. I just thought I was saving her. I scooped her up, swept her off her feet, and took her into my world.

Basically, I captured her.

That documentary showed me that, like that woman and her outlaw boyfriend, Ann went along with me when she never wanted to go along. She didn't want that kind of life. I mean, she wanted all the money and fun that came with it but not the stress, anxiety, fear, that type of thing. She didn't have the mental skills or strength to cope with that.

What Ann did instead was agree with everything, but she also kept a lot of things hidden from me, to protect my emotional state. The thing is, I couldn't see her emotional state until she left me, and I watched *Heist*. Then I got the sense of how she must have felt to be stuck in that kind of situation, and how going along with things was her only option at the time.

I had already been doing my best to look at things through her eyes and try to see her perspective. I was trying to be a friend, doing things for her, treating her like a little sister versus a romantic kind of thing, and that was helping the relationship. It was the documentary, though, that made me see what Ann had been experiencing, not what I THOUGHT she'd been experiencing. Clearly, what I thought wasn't anything like what it was simply because of where we ended up. Watching that show, I started to appreciate the severity of how frightened and trapped she was in that situation. All along, when I thought I'd been protecting Ann and putting her first, giving her the life of a princess, really what I'd done was take her into the underbelly and keep her there.

For me, because of my childhood, going through the things I brought her through didn't have the same effect. But for Ann, the two massive fires, the Hydro meter being ripped off when she was trapped in the house alone, the constant fear of rippers coming to the door—those things scared the living crap out of her. She told me she had post-traumatic stress disorder, and I never really understood that until she left.

When those things happened, I felt I was doing what I needed to do. I was taking care of her. I was making sure she didn't have to deal with any of the aftermath of what was going on. I thought I was protecting her.

Only after Ann left and I started to reflect and look at things from her perspective did I realize I was the one responsible for all this.

Only after Ann left did I begin looking at MYSELF.

She Grew Up a Jehovah's Witness but Had Underwear Tacked to Her Bedroom Wall

Ann was a light. She was funny, extremely social, and a fantastic pool player. I would have to leave the bar because I would be getting ready for a bodybuilding contest, so I'd have to get my ass home and get some sleep, and she would stay to play pool for bras and underwear. Of course I was jealous. I didn't like that. How was I supposed to like that? But she would break the cue and clean the table before anybody else ever had a chance to take another shot, and she would keep the underwear tacked to her bedroom wall.

Ann was also very artistic and a fantastic singer, but growing up in a Jehovah's Witness home, those talents were not encouraged or even allowed. They were worldly desires, and worldly desires were frowned upon in that faith. That's why she bolted at 17 years old for a life of drugs, alcohol, and partying. That's why she was drinking too much when I met her at the bar a few years later. That's what I thought I saved her from when I took her out of that life.

Instead, I brought Ann into a life of constant anxiety and fear—a life of no close friends or confidantes, where we couldn't just go anywhere and talk to anybody and have that freedom. Ann couldn't do what she loved to do or be who she really was. Me, I was quite happy sitting at home and doing my own thing, and at the time, Ann appeared to be as well.

At least, that's what I saw, or what she wanted me to see. But when she left me, saying, "I'm losing my light," this is what she meant. This is where it started.

This was what I was responsible for.

She Met a New Man

I think what got a little bit tough is when I found out that Ann had met somebody, and she was hiding the ring he had put on her finger. For me, it was like losing her all over again.

She assured me she could never see her life without me in it—meaning she still loved me, but she couldn't do the romantic thing anymore, which I get, and that's all good. But one of the areas I was failing in was I was not being very positive toward him. When I brought Ann into my life, I started taking care of her right away, and now she was struggling, and I was thinking to myself, *Where's your man? Why isn't he stepping up to help?* That sort of thing.

But once I started looking at it from her perspective and watching *the documentary*, I started changing myself. I changed my thought processes even about him. When I started to accept her boyfriend, talk about him in a positive light, and talk about them together as being great, things got even better between us.

I mean, she was my princess. I kept her on a pedestal. I still do, to this day. She lives with him now, is engaged to be married to him, and I still pay her money out of each one of my checks to make sure she's OK. I say to Ann, "I know and I trust that when you don't need my help anymore, you will tell me."

You know, it's my approach to the situation and how it affected me. I've heard from many of my friends, who've said, "You would have so much more if you stopped giving her money. She walked out on you —" all this type of stuff. And I always say, "Well, you have to realize that I'm not doing this for her. I'm doing it for me. I do this because it makes me feel good. It changes my perspective and my outlook, and it makes everything else fall into place."

Because I changed myself.

SECTION 7

How I Got The Secret Back

I t would have been one of the weekends that we were visiting Ann's dad, a couple of years after we'd gotten together. *The Secret* was something he stumbled upon and watched because he was always that type of person—work hard, follow your dreams. Because he was very close to Ann, he introduced it to us and said, "You guys should watch it. You're all about mindset and how you think and stuff like that." So yeah, we watched it all the time back then, and it made sense.

But because of the industry I was in, it was impossible for *The Secret* to work. We were basically living on the dark side, so you could think as positively as you wanted about it, but there was always that element of fear, of not knowing what could happen next.

After Ann left, and I began to see things from her POV, I asked myself questions like, *How did this all happen? What did I do to make this happen? How did I create this environment for myself?* I mean, I've always been motivated, uplifting, and positive. They call me Tony Robbins at work. So what was going on?

When all this was taking place, I was watching CNN. I was always watching CNN. Chris Cuomo, Anderson Cooper, Don Lemon—they were my buddies. Throughout my entire relationship with Ann, it was one of our go-to things we watched to stay informed. It was on so much— we were basically listening to that crap all the time. You hardly ever heard anything good, and if you did, it was either at the very end or at the very beginning for a brief moment, as a segue into something horrifying. That was the background of our life together.

After Ann left, the sadness I felt was just sort of bizarre. I was coming from a place where I thought I had my entire life completely figured out and then realized that I knew nothing about what the hell was going on, based on that one event. And CNN was not helping.

Then one night, I was browsing Netflix and noticed they had put *The Secret* back on, so I started watching it, over and over again. It's only an hour and 20 minutes long. If I was home on a Saturday, I would have it playing throughout the day, all day. Even if I wasn't necessarily sitting in front of the TV, and it was just background noise, it was on. It was something to listen to rather than hearing what was going on outside in the world, kind of thing, because I was already in a sad, sad state.

And *The Secret* helped me. *The Secret* saved me.

If You Want to Change Your Life

The conscious mind is the conduit for the subconscious mind, and when you're involved in organized crime or that type of lifestyle, you've got that in back of your mind whether you're just driving somewhere or going out for groceries. You're always thinking, *Will there be a bunch of cops at my house when I get home?* You know, that sits in the subconscious mind. You've got no control over it. The only way to change that is to change your environment.

As they say, if you want your life to change, you need to change your life, kind of thing. Right?

Obviously, I can't speak to Ann's state of mind back then; if I knew that, we'd probably still be together. But based on the life that we were living, she was always on edge, especially after the first fire. The helicopters, the rippers, all of that. Most of the other things that went on in her life were more of a distraction than anything else because she would always come back to those types of concern.

Ann was a very positive thinker. She wasn't someone who dwelled on the negative. But you could see the things that took place in our life affected her a lot differently than they did me. She was uncomfortable a lot of the time, unless she was drinking a lot, in which case she wasn't necessarily uncomfortable, but she certainly wasn't in a good state of mind, either.

And then we had CNN in the background all the time, like our unconscious mind, feeding into all the negatives in our life, accenting everything, making us think about our own horrors that we were dealing with.

Ann never wanted children because of how the world is. Even though she was a positive person with a great light and a positive outlook in the front, in the back she was dealing with all the negative stuff like everybody else. We didn't talk about it much, but we weren't avoiding it, either.

Whereas now, I avoid it because I know it's a choice.

First Heist and Then The Secret

When I found *The Secret* again, I just knew I needed to watch it. I needed to reintroduce myself to it. I was looking inside to figure out what I had done. What got me on this path? How did I end up losing what in my mind seemed to be a very perfect relationship with Ann, the love of my life?

I mean, there was no arguing, screaming, fighting, that type of thing. I always looked on the positive side of things, always tried to be happy. But I didn't realize Ann was not honest throughout a lot of it. Looking back at her emotional state in that particular lifestyle, even though she put up a good front, I think she was probably always a lot more frightened than what I saw.

What I wanted to see.

Ann and I still haven't had any deep conversations about it to this day. All I got was that five-minute explanation of her attitude toward the breakup. So I basically had to look back within myself and then see how everything unfolded from her perspective. And you know, a lot of what I did that I thought she wanted was obviously way off the mark.

The Secret is about understanding that outside circumstances are not responsible for how you feel. It's how you feel that creates the outside circumstances. *The Secret* makes you aware that your thoughts and the things that you dwell on the most become the experiences that you tend to have. It's called the law of attraction. *The Secret* forced me to realize the things that were happening to me were a result of the things I did, not things that Ann did—or anyone else, for that matter.

All along, I had held the steering wheel, and Ann was just a passenger.

But even as she reaped the rewards and the benefits, she also carried the fear and the stress and all those other types of feelings that I couldn't protect her from. I couldn't control how she responded to what happened around her.

The Secret made me understand that I was responsible for how I felt within and that how I felt was creating my circumstances. Not. The. Other. Way. Around. I understood that I had to change my mindset and how I looked at things. From my perspective, it was a complete paradigm shift, "a fundamental change in approach or underlying assumptions."

Taking it to this level has helped me in so many ways. It definitely made the relationship that I had with Ann after she left better, even though I'm not necessarily getting what I would expect from her. But I know that's because of what's going on in her environment.

I can't control the people that she's chosen to surround herself with. I can't communicate with her because her friends and the man she's marrying don't understand how we can still be on good terms after a 21-year relationship dissolved. And therein lies the thing with 95% of people— they choose to live their life blaming their feelings on the circumstance rather than recognizing that their feelings are creating that circumstance. But I don't allow that to change how I behave toward Ann.

So, that was a really big thing for me.

SECTION 8

The Greatest Unknown

I think the difference is the positive guy I was before hesitated on every action and usually didn't move forward.

I started to look back at my life as a whole and recognize all the opportunities that were presented to me as an athlete. All throughout my bodybuilding career, things were handed to me, and I turned them down because I had to work on Monday. I couldn't afford to travel. I couldn't afford this or that.

When a magazine said to me, "We need some video tape of you training," I said, "Well, how am I gonna do that? I'm not Dorian Yates. I don't have an entourage. I train by myself, so who's going to hold the camera?" I always had a negative response to the people the Universe was sending to me.

But one of the things I've learned is that the things you write down have a lot of power.

So, I used to have my pictures in pretty much every health food store and gym in the Lower Mainland, but I would sign them "greatest unknown bodybuilder of all time." I was literally writing it over and over and over again, and I posted that picture everywhere. Of course, that's the reality I experienced—being someone that everybody raved about who never did get the magazine articles, never got the photo shoots, you know what I mean?

Because that was the reality I created for myself.

Listen When the Universe Talks to You

Because of *The Secret*, I got an Audible account and began seeking out more and more authors with the same kind of message, learning how to cleanse my soul and clean my spirit by opening myself up and looking at the joy and the positive things in my life. I still listen, I'd say, a minimum of four hours a day.

Authors such as Bob Proctor, Joe Vitale, people like Napoleon Hill, W. Clement Stone, those types of guys that really take it to a whole other level, understanding how you make your life unfold and how you can actually have whatever you want in this world, if you believe and have the faith and take action when the Universe speaks to you.

With Ann, the plan was always around money. In the industry, you wanted to make as much money as you possibly could in the shortest period of time because it was a lifestyle that you didn't want to have to stay in forever. Let's just say, many legitimate businesses that exist right now started on the back of criminal activity.

You wanted to have enough money to invest, to do something with, in order to put yourself in a situation where you didn't have to go to work every day or you could work at something you loved and not have to worry about how much money you made, that sort of thing. That was the goal then because in that environment, the longer you stayed, the greater the risk of something horrible happening…as I can obviously speak to with my own experience.

Now my life is about wealth, a full range of abundance, not just money.

When I was a premiere bodybuilder, I had that mental focus; I had that mental power because I was actually a very good athlete. I was utilizing *The Secret* in those circumstances to get me up on the stage for those competitions. However, when the Universe was putting things and opportunities in place for me off the stage, I kept rejecting them based on my attitude.

Now, when I have an idea, when something comes to me, I act on it. For me, it's the whole aspect of moving forward, regardless of the fear and the anxiety. I choose "what if…" up, not "what if…" down.

Like I described it to a friend of mine, "I don't sit still anymore."

I'm acting on my inspired thoughts, starting to have ideas that are positive, uplifting, and motivating versus ideas of crappy things in my life. I'm focusing on the things that I want versus thinking about the things that I don't want. What I'm beginning to understand is that I can get much more if I pursue much more, if I change my outlook and my perspective, the attitudes, and the mentality that I was raised with. Things like "if you work hard you'll get it. If you do this and if you do that…blah blah blah" when really it's having and acting on your inspired thoughts.

And this awareness has affected all the areas of my life.

One day, I was at a meeting at work and the owner was talking about drivers washing concrete to the ground, the effects to the environment and all the fines it was causing. That inspired me to think about something I could do about that. I brought the idea to my employer, who said he thought it was a fantastic idea. Then as I left the plant, there was a little voice in my head saying why, when we give you a million dollar idea, do you give it to somebody else?

When I came back from my next load I said, "You know what? Forget about talking to the owner for me. I'll get something together for him myself." And I sought out a company that would actually be able to bring this to the forefront.

Now when I have an idea, I act on it.

Most of the changes that have taken place since Ann left me are emotional and how I feel about my future now, as opposed to how I felt about the future with her that I lost. For me, that means being able to talk to Ann and not be angry, not be mad about her new guy. You know, I tried to change my perspective on him for a long time, but it wasn't until I started to give him the respect that he deserved—and that I should be giving any person, for that matter—that she softened in her attitudes toward me.

When I made that shift.

But I would have never made that shift if Ann hadn't left me.

Then and Now

Before, in my mind, I was always a positive, motivated, optimistic kind of guy. Even when crops were bad and things were going crappy, I was always still trying to look at the upside of the situation. But I was still heavily in the industry and nothing good was happening, even though I thought I was following the law of attraction that *The Secret* talks about. Never in my wildest dreams back then would I have been doing all the stuff I'm doing now. Like I never thought I would be in my 50s and write a book. So that's what really changed for me in the biggest way when I say I lost the love of my life and became wealthy as a result.

Why did I want to write this book? People asked me that, and I told them, "Because it had been eating at me for a good two weeks. Every time I went to bed, a voice in my head just kept saying, 'You should write this. You should write this. You should write about this.' And I thought to myself, *That's the Universe, knocking on my door, saying, 'Here's an opportunity to bring additional income into your life.'*" But it's not only that. I wanted to share what I've learned and hopefully give somebody else a different perspective.

What I'm finding about myself is if I'm in a situation where I can be talking to somebody, helping them feel better about themselves or whatever it is they're doing, I kind of light up inside a little bit. It's the same as when I was a personal trainer many years ago, and when I helped people with their nutrition because I'm a certified nutrition specialist as well. You know, when I helped people with all this type of stuff, I was always at my very best. I always felt great when I was taking somebody and lifting them up.

And that's how I feel about my life now.

Even just in my day to day as a concrete truck driver, I get things that irritate me on a regular basis; it's long hours, it's a lot of pressure, but every day is great. I remember I was in my dispatch office and I grabbed one of our tickets and looked at it and it said Bosa, one of the big companies that we work with. I went, "Yay, one of my favorite jobs!" and my supervisor looked at me and said, "You sure know how to make your supervisor feel good." And I said, "Well, honestly, even if the concrete is dry and everything is going wrong, it's still the best job ever."

That's how I have a good day every day.

It's called the paradigm shift. That's what I'm doing. I still have homework to do, which is basically writing out my money biography, writing out what I want to be and what I want to have. Just the same effect that writing on the picture of me had, but in a positive way. And on the wall in my bedroom is a check for $5 million. It's not a real check, but every night before I go to bed, I look at that check for $5 million because that's what I want to go to sleep thinking about. It's that number because I like that number. I think everybody likes that number.

It's one of those things—understanding and having the awareness that everything is available to you. It's being aware of your emotional responses and knowing that you're responsible for all the events in your life.

I'm not a motivational speaker, but I play one in real life because I spend a lot of time talking to other people about this very subject. I don't want to be talking about negative stuff either. If I'm sitting with somebody and they bring up a negative topic, I'm going to try to put a positive spin on it, make it funny. If someone complains about the price of gas, I say, "Well, the good news is you spend the same amount of money but you're only there for half the time!" As silly as it seems, it's just trying to make somebody realize you can't let your life unfold based on things you have no control over, but you can control your thoughts to create the life that you want.

It's funny. If I was still with Ann, it would have been just like everybody else. We would have discussed everything I wanted to do but it would have never been acted on. It would have always been the case of " How could we afford to do that?" Well, I don't have bags of money hanging off the doorknobs in my house right now but the end picture is what I need to focus on. That's my choice.

That's the reality of the life I'm creating for myself now.

In the End

She's probably the first girl that ever said that she loved me before I said that I loved her. Wow, that was a big deal for me.

When Ann and I first came together, I think I made her feel a lot more secure, and she helped me as well. I used to be a very angry guy and a lot of that left me, because of the type of person she was. We helped each other a lot. Then when we were in lockdown all those years, whenever I left, the gate was locked and she was always scared, but when she was with me, she still had that sense of security. Somewhere along the line, she stopped feeling that way, and I didn't see it.

Like I said, when she left me, I was blindsided. You know, I was always moving forward, I didn't look at the bad, I only tried to focus on the good, but when that happened, I was lost and confused. I didn't understand what was going on. To have somebody that you spent 21 years elevating and building a life with do something like that—it's the ultimate betrayal.

It's the ultimate rejection.

Initially, I did rant and rave a little bit, but then I realized I couldn't change her. I couldn't make her want to be with me. All I could do was change myself and try to see it from Ann's POV. Doing that while opening my mind and my heart to the law of attraction is when I began to finally understand what was going on. I began to see that it's your mind that creates your environment and not the other way around. You're responsible for your own life. Your circumstances are an inside job, and you're the only one with the power to fix it.

And deep down inside of me, I always knew it.

Why else, when Ann broke up with me, would the first thing in my head be what Jane had told me 21 years before—that I would never have a successful relationship because I had never been my own person? Why else would I have said to myself, *Wow, you were right?*

Things happen to make us better.

I thought I had the most perfect relationship ever with Ann. She was my princess, and I thought we would be together forever. Obviously, that was not the case. But as a result of what happened, it brought me to a point in my life where I could not only see the things I did in the past to sabotage myself, I'm more aware of things that pop into my head now that I don't want to have there.

Things happen to make us better; they don't happen to make us worse. Things that make a big impact happen to give us the strength to get out of that negative state, that state of depression. It's by changing your attitude, your mindset.

Like what happened with Ann. It could have gone horribly, still connected to a certain degree by the condo we own and having to carry on. But when I tell people the things I do for her even now, years later, they look at me like I'm out of my mind. Why are you doing that for her after what she did to you? And I tell the truth: I'm not doing it for her. I'm doing it for me.

If you want your life to change, you have to change your life.

We have to recognize that we've been given the ability to make our own decisions and to have free will. If we choose to be angry and upset and live in a negative energy, we're going to attract negative circumstances; if we live in a positive world and try to see what good can come from whatever the situation is, then you really have a different feeling. It creates a different energy.

Now, I have a positive relationship with Ann. The new people around her can't understand how we could go from having a 21-year relationship to being friends and being able to communicate without arguing and fighting, but I know it's because it's like we're on another level. We can respect each other and have this together because we get it.

I'm sharing this story with you because I want you to get it too. I want you to know it can be done. I want you to understand that even in the darkest situations, looking for the positive, looking for the light is what will bring you out and bring you to the next level of yourself.

When I first met Ann, she was such a light it was like you could actually see the glow, she was so bright. Twenty-one years later, when she told me she was losing it and she had to go, I was devastated.

But you know what?

It was never about what Ann had or didn't have. My life was about me and how I was so afraid of my OWN light, I used to sign my picture "the greatest unknown bodybuilder of all time." I was anonymous, even to myself, but it took Ann leaving me to realize that.

If you see your story in mine, then you will understand what I'm really sharing with you: The very worst thing that can happen to you can also be the very best thing if you see it from a different perspective, like I've learned to do.

Awareness has become the biggest thing for me. To recognize when something is having a negative impact on my emotions and being able to change that. It gives me a day to day happy life. Awareness is the thing that saved me from the worst heartbreak I never thought I would recover from and has been the catalyst for me becoming my greatest self.

I did it. You can do it too.

Look for the light.

DEDICATIONS

I would like to dedicate this book to Rhonda Byrne, Joe Vitale, Jack Canfield, Bob Proctor, John Assaraf, Michael B Beckwith, James Arthur Ray, John Hagelin, Morris Goodman, Denis Waitley, Marci Shimoff, Hale Dwoskin, Lee Brower, Neale Donald Walsch, Lisa Nichols, John F Demartini, David Schirmer , Loral Langemeier, Bill Harris, John Gray, Bob Doyle, Mike Dooley, Marie Diamond.

A special thanks to the cast of The Secrct who were instrumental in changing most everything in my life.

In fond memory of Bob Proctor: how does one have such an impact on so many people's lives? Well, I don't know. However, I will say this, I personally was heavily influenced by Bob's work, and although I never had the pleasure of meeting him, I listened to him almost daily. As a result of his teachings, I wrote this book.

I couldn't wait to send a signed copy to him so I could hear his feedback, whatever that may have been. Learning of his passing halfway through writing was a bit heartbreaking but like he taught me, I moved forward.

Since I won't be hearing back from Bob, I'd like to share my own feelings: You're a great man. I wish I had met you. Thank you for your words, what you taught and how you taught it. Thanks now for making heaven a better place for the rest of us when we get there.

Bless you and yours, Bob.

Finally, for Carlene Marshall:

It wasn't easy for you, trying to break down the walls I had built up because of my experiences, but you held on even when it seemed it wasn't going to work out.

Adding to the mix was me writing this book, highlighting the great love I had lost and then asking you to proofread it. I'm sure to some degree it gave you a sense of inadequacy and it was probably pretty hurtful, yet Carlene, you still did what I asked, stood behind me and pushed me forward.

I want to say thank you and let you know that in the short time we've been together, you've shown me more love than I've received in a lifetime. I love you for that and I want you to know that it's really me that needs to live up to you

Tommy Thompson
August 19, 2022

Story Terrace

www.ingramcontent.com/pod-product-compliance
Lightning Source LLC
Chambersburg PA
CBHW030042100526
44590CB00011B/307